CW01192425

the single front wheel was a conventional motor-cycle unit mounted on sprung forks controlled by handlebars inside the cabin of the van body, which had a carrying capacity of 7cwt. One of Tom's former colleagues at Raleigh, E.S. 'Tommo' Thompson, joined his enterprise in October 1934 and by using hand-drilling machines, files and hacksaws they produced the first chassis. Machining work had to be farmed out, while a friendly local garage offered space for assembly of the prototype, which first took to the road on 1 January 1935.

While Thompson concentrated on the assembly process, Tom Williams found suitable premises at the recently abandoned Midland Red Omnibus Co. garage on the main A5, which he leased for 14 years. An added bonus was the existence of two 1,000 gallon petrol tanks on to which electric pumps were soon installed to achieve a small income from petrol sales while vehicle production commenced. After only six months' occupation the first van was delivered on 3 March 1935 and a month later the Reliant Engineering Co. Ltd was formed. Another ex-Raleigh manager, Mr Bridcutt, joined Reliant as Sales Director.

It soon became apparent that more refinement was needed, with more carrying capacity – so a V-Twin JAP engine was adopted, now driving the leaf-sprung spiral bevel rear axle by shaft. The first example of this pattern was sold on 26 March 1936 and shortly afterwards the directors decided to produce their own aluminium bodywork to eliminate the cost and possible damage of transportation. The need for more power and further refinement prompted Tom Williams to approach the Industrial department of the Austin Motor Co. at the 1937 Commercial Motor Show regarding the use of their Austin 7 engine and gearbox in his three-wheeled vans. Fortunately the Birmingham company agreed and within three months a 8cwt capacity van had been built using the 747cc 4-cylinder water-cooled Austin engine, offering a much smoother and quieter power source. The deal with Austin included the supply of complete power units fitted with carburettor, fuel pump, starter and dynamo. This enabled production to be increased to the extent that additional premises were acquired to house the bodywork assembly plant. The whole Two Gates site at Tamworth was purchased freehold in June 1939 after 1,000 vans had been produced there, before war broke out three months later. This initial success certainly answered the criticisms by many of the pundits about the viability of three-wheeled vehicles. Undoubtedly the economy of licensing and fuel consumption linked to excellent manoeuvrability were the attractive qualities to the increasing numbers of customers.

However, Reliant were soon to receive their first body blow in late 1938 when rumours of Austin's intention to abandon production of the 747cc engine came true, leaving the young Tamworth company with no power source for their vehicles. Reliant had little option but to try and produce their own engines and gearboxes based on the Austin unit. This proved to be one more step in Reliant's history of becoming almost entirely self-sufficient in their manufacturing ability. With the onset of war many machining firms were preoccupied with producing armaments, so Reliant set up their own machining facilities, which came into further use during the hostilities when they produced over 1½ million components for the War Ministry.

While setting up production of their own 750cc engine Reliant made a number of improvements, including chain drive to the camshaft and gear driven oil pump and distributor. The first home-built engines left the line a week after war started in

September 1939, although they did not come into production until 1946. The war effort allowed Reliant to establish a comprehensive machining operation, but some of Reliant's premises had been commandeered for War Ministry purposes so another body assembly building had to be built. Despite this, the first post-war vehicle was delivered on 13 March 1946.

In June of that year a very significant figure, Tom Scott, joined Reliant fresh from serving in the RAF. He entered the sales department and within a year was Sales Manager, a post he held until his retirement nearly 30 years later. At the same time E.S. Thompson was promoted to Works Director as a reward for his previous 12 years' service. In order to further their manufacturing independence, Reliant acquired a small gear-cutting firm, Morson Engineering of Coventry, in 1948. The following year the machine shop was expanded ready for the introduction of the Regent van in 1950, with further improvements including cheaper and stronger steel wheels. No fewer than 3,000 of this latest model were produced during the following six years when production of the range ceased. This brought the total number of commercial vehicles since the company had started 21 years previously to 5,834 by the time production ended in 1956.

The choice of aluminium for the bodywork of the vans was beneficial for two reasons. First, it was light and easy to work with, which was essential when attempting to produce a lightweight vehicle by hand forming methods. Secondly, the availability of aluminium post-war was not restricted in the same way as steel, for which allocations were made on the basis of how big a proportion of the production volume was exported – the 'export or die' principle. The latter condition would have proved a great problem for Reliant who had virtually no export market at that stage.

The versatile Regent vans were used for a fascinating variety of applications, from conventional closed delivery vehicles to drop-sided mobile grocery shops, milk floats and even open-sided passenger carriers. This last application of the three-wheeler format might well have sparked off the idea of producing passenger cars, harking back to the days when Tom Williams was working for Raleigh.

The very first private effort by Tom Williams to produce a three-wheeled commercial vehicle in the back garden of his home at Tamworth, 1934. A Raleigh motorcycle front fork system is evident, while the wooden load platform at the rear was no doubt temporary. The chassis construction too looks somewhat experimental.

By 1938 about ten vans a week were leaving this elevated assembly platform. An overhead gantry probably lowered complete body units, made by an outside concern, on to the rolling chassis at the stage of production shown here. The ramp at the right indicates that this is virtually the end of the assembly line, which was only about 100 ft long.

A 1950 van with a carrying capacity of 10cwt, the largest ever made by Reliant. It was now powered by Reliant's own engine based on the previous Austin 7 unit. Slotted steel wheels were used possibly for strength reasons, as well as being more economical now that such items could be stamped on modern steel presses.

The coachbuilt nature of the Reliant vans is clearly seen in this pre-war example, with the aluminium panelling supported by a complex ash frame. The bulge beside the solo driver's seat shows the intrusion made by the 4-cylinder engine, which was easily accessible from inside the cabin by removing the cover in front of the gear lever.

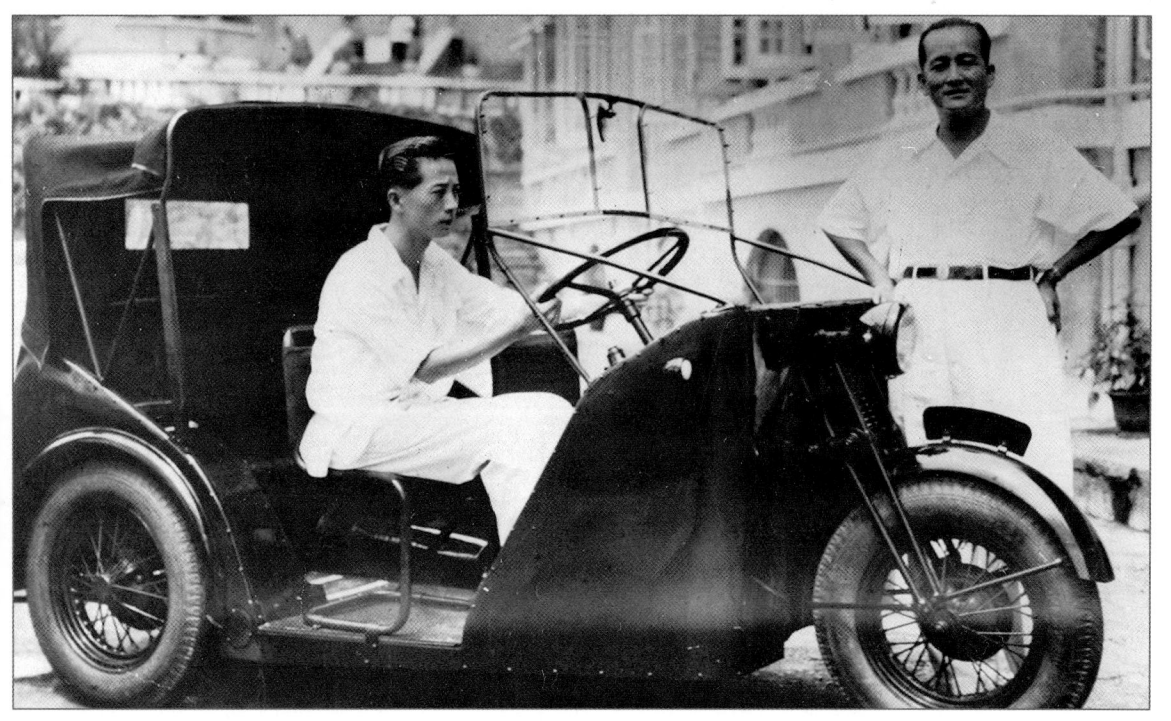

This fascinating rickshaw adaption of a Reliant chassis in use somewhere in the Far East exemplifies the versatility of the basic design. Its compactness and manoeuvrability made it ideal for town use. Presumably this was a local version as no records exist of Reliant producing such a carriage.

The Reliant-built, 747cc side valve engine introduced in 1939 was based on the previously employed Austin 7 unit which went out of production in 1938. Austin were perfectly happy for Tom Williams to pinch the design, and Reliant incorporated improvements such as a chain driven camshaft, oil pump and distributor drive.

Another example of the 10cwt van built in 1950, proving an ideal delivery vehicle in urban situations. There cannot have been many more economical means of commercial transport in towns at the time and their tiny turning circle must have been a boon in traffic.

This mobile grocery shop is a cunning piece of design known as the Regent 10cwt Mobile Shop or 'Veg-e-Car' as the headboard signifies. The price, excluding fittings that would have been made up locally, was £295 plus £32 9s 5d purchase tax, with a 10–14 day delivery period.

This small firm had clearly just bought both pick-up and van versions of the 1950 Regent model, judging from the consecutive registration numbers. These two vehicles were probably intended for delivery and servicing the owner's products in and around town, although covering rural areas would not have been a problem.

construction followed the same principle as the vans, comprising hand beaten aluminium panels supported on an ash framework.

The Regal Mk I was produced only in drophead format, with accommodation for two adults and two children. A total of 145 examples were made in 1953 and a further 855 in 1954, before the Mk II was introduced later that year, with cleaner lines and a glass fibre hardtop. Two years later, at the instigation of Tom Scott, the Sales Director, all the external bodywork of the new Mk III version of the Regal was made from moulded glass fibre, still mounted on an ash frame. The Mk III Regal now proved competitive in performance with similarly powered four-wheeled cars yet only required a motor cycle licence to drive it, coupled with a reduced road fund licence applicable to all cars with only three wheels weighing less than 8cwt. The following *Motor* road test figures show the relative performance of the 1957 Mk III compared with contemporary four-wheeled, four-seater saloon cars:

Marque	Price	Weight	cc	0–50 mph	20–40 mph in top	Max. mph	mpg
Regal	£430	8 cwt	747	25.5s	15.3s	59.9	46.5
Fiat 600	£585	11 cwt	633	32.5s	27.2s	58.3	44.7
Goggomobile	£671	12 cwt	688	28.5s	15.6s	66.0	43.8
Standard 8	£554	14 cwt	803	27.7s	17.6s	62.1	37.3

Comparisons with other three-wheelers are not relevant as they had much smaller engines, as in the case of the Bond Minicar, which could carry only two people, or the BMW Isetta.

Thus we can see that the Regal Mk III was at least £100 cheaper than the comparable four-wheelers and enjoyed an annual road tax of only £5 compared with £12 10s for these four-wheelers in 1957. When *Motor* tested this Reliant they mentioned how well it held its own in normal traffic, much to the surprise of other drivers. They also commented that the steering seemed unduly direct, but drivers soon became accustomed to this feature, and stability was adequate when driven sensibly. The testers did find the noise level rather excessive, largely owing to the position of the engine and gearbox virtually between the front seats.

The much smoother body shape of the Mk III no doubt helped its sales to equal the total sales of both the previous models. Further small refinements such as wind-up windows were added when the Mk IV arrived with a very similar overall shape. However a thorough redesign to produce the Mk V with a more stylish and sharper bodystyle further established Reliant in the three-wheeler market, selling no fewer than 4,770 saloons as well as over 1,000 van versions since the Regent had been discontinued in 1956. The final version of the Regal, the Mk VI, appeared in 1961, still retaining the ash framed bodywork and torsion bar front suspension but having a lengthened roof line with a lip over the rear window. This model sold even better than previous versions, attracting 8,478 customers.

The next landmark in the development of the Reliant three-wheeler hove into view in 1962, the seventh version of the Regal, which became known as the

Regal 3/25, referring to the number of wheels and the bhp of the engine. The power unit for this new model was a completely new design evolved by Ron Heathcote, consisting of a light alloy block as before but surmounted by a cylinder head of similar material featuring overhead valves and wet liners for the cylinders in the block with a capacity of only 598cc. The output of this new engine was now 24bhp compared with 17bhp for the earlier sidevalve unit. An added advantage was the low weight of the OHV unit of 138lb, so important for the three-wheeled car which must weigh less than 8cwt to qualify for a motorcycle licence. Significantly, the new Reliant engine was the first British all-alloy engine in flow-line production. The chassis of the new Regal model was also improved in strength and ease of production and now incorporated coil spring over damper front suspension in place of the previous torsion bar system. Perhaps even more significant was the design of the bodywork, which now consisted of two large glassfibre mouldings bonded together to form a rigid monocoque unit mounted on the new chassis, thus adding rigidity to the latter rather than depending on it for its integrity. Not only was this form of construction cheaper and quicker to build, it produced a car of greater rigidity and quietness. In order to attract an even bigger market for the new model, the styling featured a reverse-angle rear window similar to the contemporary Ford Anglia 105E saloon.

Despite the smaller engine capacity, the more powerful 600cc unit gave the Regal 3/25 a slightly improved performance over its predecessors, coupled now with better accommodation for four adults. The following performance figures from the 1963 *Motor* road tests show the comparison with similarly priced four-wheelers on the British market at the time:

This overhead view shows the first of the Regal passenger car rolling chassis fitted with the trusty Reliant engine and gearbox. The most radical change was abandoning the motor cycle forks at the front in favour of a forged leading arm pivoted at the rear, having a kingpin at the front end, for steering the front wheel. The geometry of the steering mechanism is also clear from this angle.

Marque	Price	Weight	cc	0–50 mph in top	20–40 mph	Max. mph	mpg
Regal 3/25	£486	8 cwt	598	25.0s	13.8s	64.0	51.5
NSU Prinz	£526	11 cwt	598	17.8s	14.9s	71.3	45.3
Fiat 500	£411	10 cwt	499	47.2s	33.0s	60.8	53.4

Testers at the time commented on the direct steering offering little self-centring, and the tendency to lift a rear wheel if swerving suddenly to the left with only the driver aboard. However, they recognised that Reliant had done a good job with improved sound-proofing, as a result of the integral GRP bodywork construction. The handily placed gear lever was also praised for its precise action. Braking was considered absolutely first class by *Motor Cycling* magazine, who also applauded the camaraderie developing among Reliant owners as increasing numbers were now appearing on British roads. Sales were now approaching 10,000 per year, and in order to maintain this success Reliant introduced the Super version at the 1965 Motor Show featuring a smoother grille on the front panel. Van versions of the 3/25 were equally successful and total sales of this model reached 63,000 by 1968. At this point the engine capacity was increased to 700cc, yielding a power output of 29bhp. In recognition of this development the Regal was now known as the 3/30, which performed against the competition as follows:

Marque	Price	Weight	cc	0–50 mph in top	20–40 mph	Max. mph	mpg
Regal 3/30	£575	8 cwt	697	15.0s	11.5s	74.0	54.5
DAF	£820	13 cwt	746	22.0s	8.6s	62.8	42.8
BMW 700	£893	12 cwt	697	17.4s	19.4s	70.4	37.8

The Regal 3/25 and 3/30 were by far the most successful Reliant models in the history of the company, selling over 105,000 examples before they were superseded by the legendary Robin.

The large rear-hinged bonnet of the Regal Mk I, as it became known, offered excellent access to the engine. The spare wheel and battery were mounted above the wheel in front of the engine. The body design was very clean and neat, and the folding hood was well equipped with windows for the benefit of rear passengers.

Not only was this the first Reliant passenger car, but it was also a full four-seater open tourer offering true family transport. This view shows the rather sparse dashboard to the right of the steering column. The luggage area was reached by folding down the rear seat backrest, while the fuel tank was below this space with the fuel filler placed in the rear panel next to the number plate.

The later Regal chassis had a modified construction ahead of the radiator to support the steering box, spare wheel and battery, which also improved safety in a front-end collision. The brake master cylinder is now outboard of the chassis side member owing to re-positioning of the pedals. The chassis box sections are of simplified construction.

A preview shot of the new Regal, complete with model driver, taken at the Earls Court Motor Cycle Show late in 1952. The large diameter of the steering wheel is immediately apparent. The steering mechanism is also clearly visible from this angle, together with the 3-wheeler bonnet mascot.

The publicity department was keen to demonstrate the Regal's family friendliness. Should the weather be untypically British one could travel hood-down and enjoy a picnic! No doubt they all groomed their hair for this picture as travelling in an open car would have ruffled even the most Brylcreemed locks.

This period cutaway diagram of the first Regal model clearly shows the position of the spare wheel above the front wheel alongside the battery. The rear seats are sited above the rear axle, making them slightly higher than the front ones, which no doubt assisted forward visibility, if not safety, for rear passengers.

The Regal Mk I was announced at the 1952 Cycle and Motor Cycle show where it was the centrepiece of the Reliant stand alongside the traditional Regent van, which was still selling strongly. Compared with surrounding exhibits the Reliant stand must have stood out well, signifying as it did the beginning of a new era.

It is customary to offer journalists and dealers an opportunity to sample new motor cars when they are announced and here unregistered new Regals on trade plates are being sent on their way by a Reliant manager for testing in the Tamworth area.

The Reliant stand at the 1955 Earls Court Motor Cycle show was even more impressive, exhibiting no fewer than three examples of the Mk II Regal. These were the soft-top standard model, the optional hard-top version on the plinth, and the van derivative in the background, left. The latter had now replaced the Regent series, ending the era of motorcycle design influence.

The Mk II Regal was basically a four-seater drophead, although it must be said that adult rear passengers did look uncomfortably vulnerable. One new feature introduced on this model was a pair of trafficators mounted on the side of each front wing, rendering hand signals unnecessary.

The Reliant stand at the 1958 Motor Cycle show, where the company was now one of the largest exhibitors. Production was totally focused on the Regal model, and this exhibit features the latest Mk IV in its various guises, including a bare rolling chassis (for the technically minded).

The Mk IV Regal rather over-emphasised the height of the hardtop needed to provide headroom for the rear seat passengers, seated well above the rear axle. However, the large doors must have made getting in and out very easy.

The Regal Mk IV chassis shows a further development of the front suspension fork design. The leading arm supporting the front wheel is a steel fabrication pivoted at the rear, where it is connected to the transverse torsion bar springing medium. The earlier design consisted of a forged arm and lever arm damper, whereas a telescopic shock absorber is now seen to be in use.

A brochure picture of the Regal Mk V, which had a much sharper and more 'confident' profile than its predecessors, enhanced by the non-standard, two-tone colour scheme. Moulded-in front and rear bumpers with chrome cappings appeared for the first time. Despite the modernisation of the bodyshape it was surprising to see the return of sliding door windows.

A frontal view of the Mk V Regal introduced in 1959 highlights the stylish, oval, recessed grille, chrome-capped front quarter bumpers and separate side and indicator lights. The full-length chrome strip along the waistline gives the impression of greater length. Sales of this model reached nearly 5,000.

This sectioned version of the Regal Mk V seen at a design exhibition with floral tributes shows clearly how the bodywork is made up of two primary glass fibre mouldings. The rear seat pans are moulded into the rear section of the body, demonstrating the versatility of this material and how it contributes to the overall rigidity of the car.

The separate rear lights on this van define it as being a Mk V, which proved very popular, like its saloon sibling, during its brief period of production in 1959 and 1960. Over 1,100 customers virtually doubled the sales of its predecessor. The number plate suggests that this was an elaborately staged publicity shot, New Zealand lamb and all.

The simple instrument panel of the Mk V and Mk VI was more stylish than earlier versions and, being symmetrical, was suitable for either right- or left-hand drive. Small fuel and temperature gauges featured in the bottom segments of the large round central speedometer.

Production of the Regal models continued in the same buildings as the Regent vans, where Mk VI saloons are shown being assembled in 1961. Thanks to the glass fibre bodyshell now being made by Reliant, fewer staff were needed to produce each vehicle than before.

The final stage of the Mk VI assembly line, where the finishing touches to the bodywork are being carried out, including glass cleaning, under the eagle eye of a quality inspector.

A profile of the Mk VI saloon shows clearly the main distinguishing feature of this model: the lip above the rear window, which sharpens up the roofline and so matches the front- and rear-end shapes more closely.

The front of the Mk VI Regal at the 1960 Motor Cycle show seems identical to that of the Mk V, except for the reversion to single sidelights incorporating the winking indicator again. A more drastic modification to the rear bodywork is not evident in this photo.

The rear view of the Mk VI Regal emphasises the overhanging lip above the rear window. Also clearly shown is the external lid to the separate luggage compartment, an innovation pioneered by Reliant. This feature first appeared on the Mk V. The integral rear light cluster design had been 'borrowed' for the new model from the BLMC Minivan.

World motor racing champion Jim Clark visited Reliant in November 1963 to open the new £500,000 engineering factory at Shenstone. He is seen here standing between Tom Williams, founder and managing director of Reliant and E.S. Thompson, the works director, far right. Mr Fishwick, the local Barclays Bank manager (remember them?) is on the left of the picture.

This interior view of the new, purpose-built Shenstone plant opened by Reliant in 1963, about 5 miles from the Two Gates factory, shows the engine building area where every part of the little power unit was machined and assembled in-house. Machine guards, hairnets and other modern safety items are conspicuously absent. Reliant made over 80 per cent of their own componentry, more than any other UK manufacturer.

Reliant three-wheelers were especially favoured by city councils for urban duties. This impressive line-up of five Mk VI vans owned by Huddersfield Council demonstrates the popularity of this model, which more than trebled the sales of the previous version.

Another period publicity shot of the Mk VI Regal, emphasising its touring abilities for families of four together with their holiday equipment. Each new version of the Regal proved more popular than the last and the Mk VI sold no fewer than 8,478 saloons, almost double the sales of the Mk V, despite both models only being in production for a year.

The growing sales success of each Regal model might have led Reliant to rest on its laurels. Fortunately, management was far from complacent and the dramatic new model (of car, I mean!) shown here appeared in 1963. It was effectively the Mk VII, but was called the Regal 3/25, referring to the number of wheels and the bhp of the new OHV engine.

The new 3/25 Regal, showing off its dramatic new roofline with the reverse angle rear window copied from contemporary Ford Anglia and Classic saloons. What is not evident is the advanced method of body construction, which was now entirely glass fibre, adding further rigidity to the chassis as well as making production much simpler.

This 3/25 rolling chassis outside the Tamworth works shows two significant developments over its predecessors. The engine is now an entirely new all-alloy OHV 600cc unit designed by Reliant engineers to replace the venerable side valve unit used since 1939. And the front wheel is now supported by a coil spring rather than the previous torsion bar system.

Reliant were not slow to target large fleet users with the advantages of their three-wheelers, particularly the van versions. This 3/25 van is on trial in Hertfordshire with the AA. Clearly the use of Reliant vehicles in this demanding role would give added confidence to prospective buyers.

The Regal shown here was run by Reliant for publicity and development purposes and in January 1963 was used to follow the Monte Carlo rally in which Reliant had three works-entered Sabre 4 sports cars. The 3/25 was driven by Cecil Sandford and David Cooper and completed the whole route without any problems.

An unlikely visitor to the Reliant factory in 1963 was 25-year-old Craig Breedlove. Craig was on a world celebrity tour and had travelled from London to sample the Reliant three-wheelers, having earlier unofficially broken the world land speed record in a jet-powered three-wheel car known as 'Spirit of America': not a Reliant, I hasten to add!

342 ENX parked outside the Reliant offices, 15 August 1963. Traffic conditions in those halcyon days allowed this apparently casual photo to be taken, as the car is blocking the inside lane of the main A5 trunk road! This particular vehicle was being seen off with drivers Cyril 'Flash' Rogers and Eric Hardy on an expedition to the Sahara desert as one of its endurance tests.

Cyril Rogers poses with the gallant Regal some 300 miles into the Sahara desert. Fortunately for accurate navigation, there are maps on either door. 'Flash' was accompanied by Eric Hardy, both drivers being ex-racing motorcyclists. They achieved an average speed of 46.22 mph which, together with the luggage on the roof, contributed to the rather 'high' fuel consumption figure of 42.68 mpg.

342 ENX is seen here in Pall Mall, London being greeted by sales director, Tom Scott, on its successful return from a 5,211 mile proving run to the Sahara Desert and the high Atlas mountains, taking 16 days. The engine consumed only two pints of oil and one of water during the entire journey. The doormen outside the RAC club seem unimpressed and are obviously not expecting a tip!

At the 1965 Motor Show Reliant introduced a more luxurious version of the Regal, restyled by Ogle, known as the 3/25 Super. Surprisingly, the price of the new model at £486 was the same as the earlier version, which was retained in the range as the 3/25 Standard costing £18 less. The main external difference was the neater and more streamlined front grille.

In 1965 BOAC purchased six Regal 3/25 vans to speed internal mail and parcels around the 4½ square miles of London Heathrow airport. They replaced previous Reliant vans as well as other makes, and were photographed in squadron formation in front of a VC 10 airliner.

World Champion racing driver Jack Brabham visited the Reliant factory in 1965 and is caught here talking to Managing Director Ray Wiggin beside the production line of the increasingly popular 3/25 Regal Super, seen here with its engine cover raised.

A view of an extremely busy production line of the Regal 3/25 Super at Two Gates. By 1966 output was running at 15,000 vehicles per year. This figure gradually rose to 25,000, no fewer than 68 Regals a day!

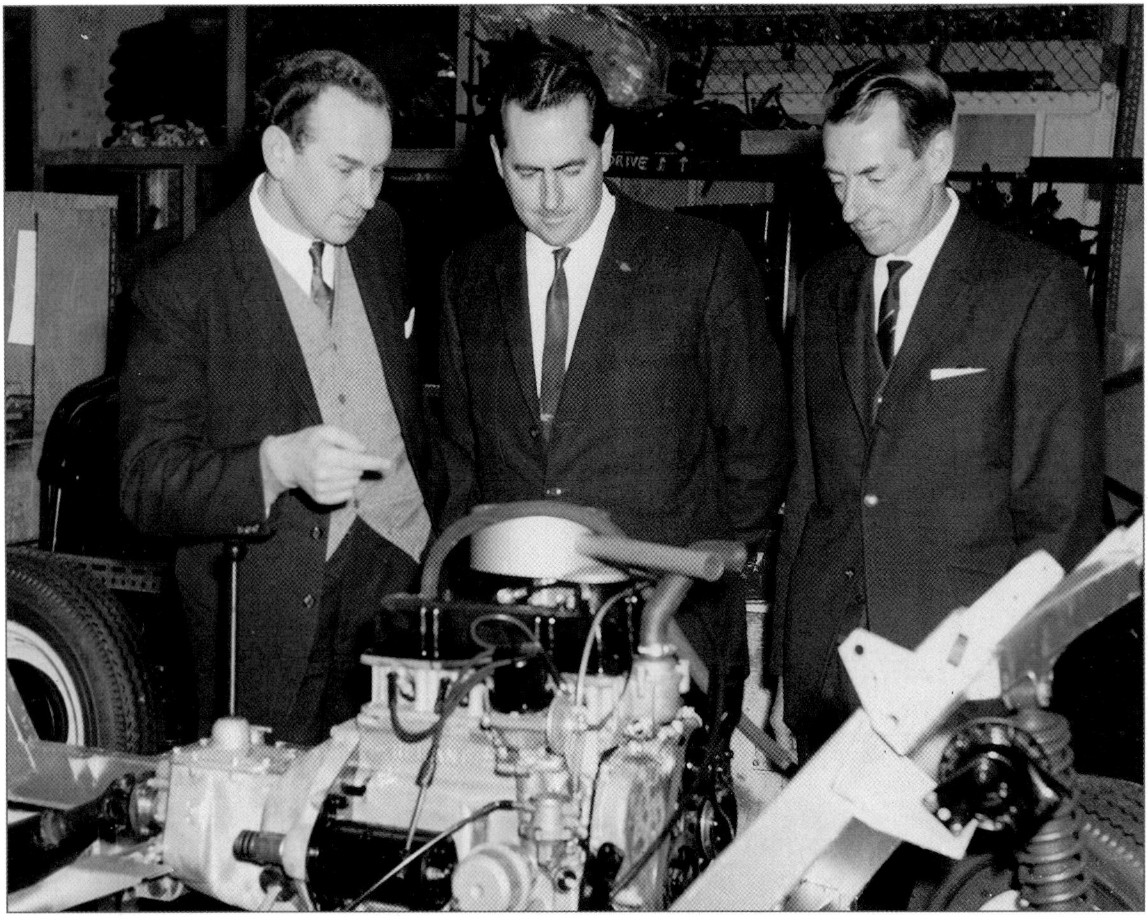

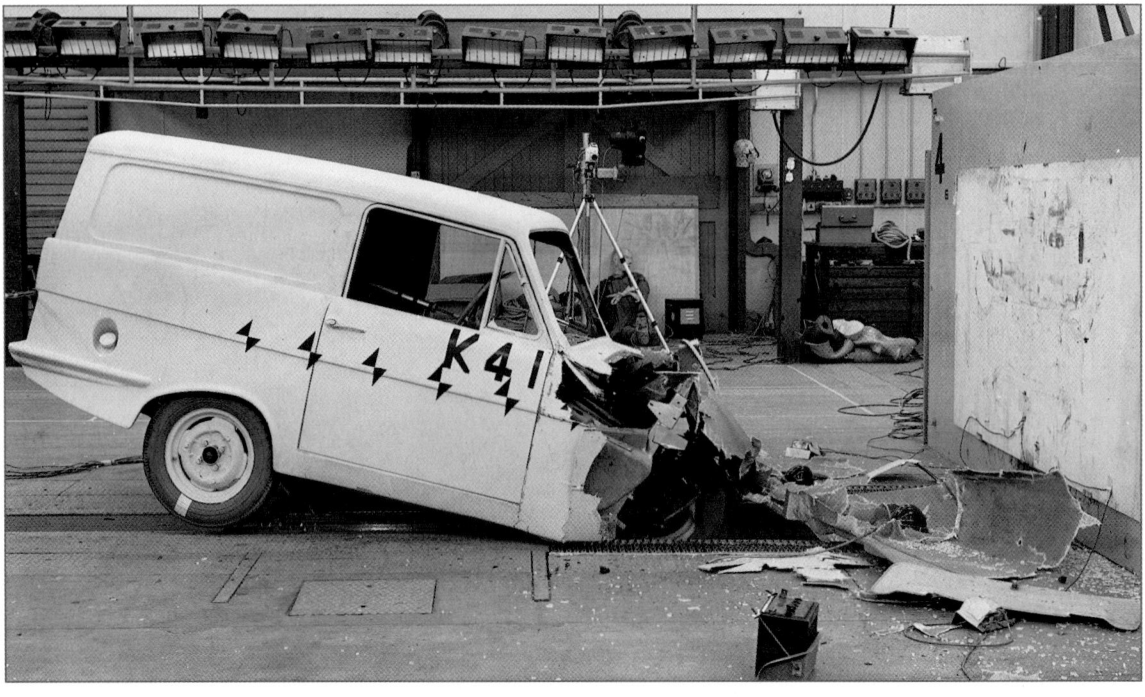
K41

Fire engulfs the Tamworth body shop, 1966. Within hours Reliant had completed the purchase of a new 70,000 sq ft factory at nearby Kettlebrook. Full production resumed in the new premises within a few weeks thanks to the 'Dunkirk' spirit of the staff and management.

Opposite, above: Ray Wiggin, on the left, shows Australian world motor racing champion Jack Brabham and his Chief Designer Ron Tauranac the chassis of a Regal 3/30 at Tamworth in 1966. The great driver said he found the visit fascinating, though the only feature Reliants shared with his racing cars was the glass fibre bodywork.

Opposite: A Regal van has been subjected to a frontal impact test. This dramatic shot illustrates how successfully glass fibre absorbs such treatment without transferring the damage to the rest of the structure. This is clearly evident from the shut lines of the driver's door being even. The chassis design also prevents the engine moving back into the passenger compartment.

50000
50,000th Regal 3/25
RELIANT

RELIANT
50000
50,000th Regal 3/25
RELIANT

A record of some sort was established at an economy meeting at Mallory Park in 1968, when 16 people crammed into the back of a Regal van and drove round the circuit, emphasising the capacious 50 cu ft of load space. In this case, the 5cwt limit would certainly have been exceeded. Another Regal saloon exceeded 100mpg at the same meeting.

Opposite, above: This historic photo captures the excitement and pride of the moment when Reliant workers carried out the 50,000th Regal 3/25, in June 1968. Sales director Tom Scott is seated in the car while Managing Director Ray Wiggin stands beside the driver's door looking justifiably pleased. This production landmark was achieved in only five years.

Opposite: As the 50,000th Regal 3/25 leaves the assembly line, sales director Tom Scott is seen shaking hands with George Jenkins, senior assembly shops foreman, appropriately dressed in a white coat. The obvious enthusiasm of the assembly workers is apparent in the background.

This detailed shot taken in the newly built Shenstone facility shows the latest crankshaft grinding equipment being operated as part of the complete engine construction operation carried out there.

Engines were assembled by hand. Some of the operatives seem rather young, apprentices perhaps. It was quite common for fathers and sons to be working together at Reliant as it was the largest employer in the Tamworth area and employed a fiercely loyal, local workforce.

This impressive line-up of finished all-alloy Reliant engines at Shenstone is ready for despatch down the A5 to the Two Gates factory for installing in the current range of three- and four-wheelers. The gearboxes were also assembled at Shenstone from parts machined in the same factory.

While most of the glass fibre bodywork was laid up by hand in open moulds certain panels, such as door skins and bonnets, were machine-pressed. Flat sheets of resin-impregnated glass fibre mat were cut into shapes to be formed in heated presses, ensuring accurate and rapid production of these components. The use of common doors and bonnets in the various models made production more economical.

Reliant not only built the bodyshells and running gear for their vehicles in-house, but they also produced all the interior panels, seats and upholstery for each model in the Two Gates factory. The seat trimming area uses tubular steel frames made up in a neighbouring unit.

The end of the Regal 3/25 Super assembly line, where the final inspection took place before a short trial run round the factory grounds was conducted on every model. Output by now was nearing 100 per day with a workforce of about 2,500.

This happy scene from 1972 records the production of the 100,000th Regal Mk VII, which in this instance was an April Yellow 3/30 saloon powered by a 700cc version of the alloy engine giving 29bhp. The designer of this famous engine, Ron Heathcote, is seen in the foreground next to the car.

The Regal 21E was so named because it was the luxury version of the Regal 3/30 and had 21 extras added. These included metallic paint, chromed hub caps and bumper overriders, bonnet and boot hinges, ammeter and oil pressure gauges – as well as a spare wheel! This model sold at £583, £64 more than the de luxe Saloon.

A publicity profile shot taken in Drayton Manor park, near the Two Gates factory, demonstrating the uncanny similarity of the rear section of the Regal bodywork to the Ford Anglia 105E. The rear bumper overriders and chrome window trims on this 21E are visible from this angle.

Fourteen million ATV viewers saw this Regal 3/30 saloon being presented to the hapless winner of a *Golden Shot* contest in 1969. The car was introduced by the show's compère, comedian Bob Monkhouse, himself later to become a notable Bond Bug enthusiast, and was presented by the actor Patrick Cargill, seen here.

Reliant optimistically featured a 21E van version in its price list, obviously intended for the more up-market shop or business where smart appearance was at a premium. Twin spotlights and chrome mirrors are the main identifying features in this frontal view, but the van also had chrome wheel trims, chrome fuel filler cap, and extra ammeter and oil pressure gauges on the dashboard to keep drivers amused.

The versatility of the Regal van is demonstrated by this unusual (and from a PR point of view, rather inadvisable) picture of one towing a trailer carrying a Regal saloon. One presumes this was to illustrate the potential of the van rather than the likely use to which it might have to be be put! Note that the specially adapted trailer needs three ramps for three-wheeler carrying.

This impressive park full of newly produced Regals of various types features the first batch of left-hand-drive pick-ups destined for Greece in 1966. Thanks to a visit by Sales Director Tom Scott, Reliant also sold 100 left-hand-drive Regal saloons and vans to Holland within the first year of exporting to Europe.

An underbonnet view of a Regal prototype demonstrating an electric motor fitted to an experimental vehicle. Reliant were clearly thinking far ahead even in the environmentally challenged 1960s, since electrically powered economy cars are only now just beginning to interest the world's major manufacturers.

The Regal back seat is fully occupied by lead acid batteries to power the front mounted electric motor. Clearly such a vehicle could only be considered as a two-seater as placing such a mass in the rear boot would severely unbalance the car.

This Regal traffic jam outside Buckingham Palace was created by the winter meeting of the London and Surrey branches of the Reliant Owners Club in 1971. Most of the models appear to be 3/25s but the occasional earlier Mk VI can also be seen. Modern traffic conditions would make such a gathering impossible nowadays.

The Reliant three-wheelers have always engendered great camaraderie among their owners, many of whom are members of the Reliant Owners Club. Meetings of members as with many motor clubs usually take place at local public houses and it is likely that these three Mk VI owners are attending such a gathering.

3
The Robin is Branded

The first Reliant Robins arrive at Goodwood race track for testing by journalists. Note the RMC registration plates used on a succession of Reliant vehicles on their announcement. The twin spotlights indicate these are top of the range models as one would expect on such occasions.

Despite the outstanding success of the Regal models, particularly the 3/25 and 3/30 of the Mk VII, of which over 100,000 were produced by 1962, Reliant were not prepared to rest on their laurels. Wisely, they planned to revamp their popular range of three-wheelers before the customers became bored with them, when sales would begin to decline. Having established a relationship with Ogle Design which had led to the introduction of the Scimitar Coupé and subsequently the very successful Scimitar GTE, it was only natural for the same designers to be called in to restyle Reliant's economy range. So it was that the Robin was hatched from the Letchworth designers' nest of talent in the form of a highly chic, one-box design, forsaking a conventional separate luggage compartment but adopting the hatchback format of the Scimitar range. A professional launch 'do' was arranged, with leading media personalities such as Raymond Baxter, into a receptive market hungry for a stylish version of their favourite range of cars. The main market for three-wheelers, as always, was exmotor-cyclists with young families, and retired couples – with the emphasis on sales in the Midlands and north of England. Reliant had built up a hugely loyal market for its cars and many owners were on their third or fourth car by the time the Robin appeared. This loyalty was apparent by the sales of the new model, which topped 10,000 in the first year of production, 1974, and no fewer than 15,000 were sold in 1975. The rate of production was about 330 per week by mid-1974. In January and February of 1975 dealers were reporting an increasing number of buyers trading in four-wheelers such as Escorts, Vivas and Minis in favour of the Robin. The reasons for this included the rust-free bodywork, leading to reduced maintenance and depreciation, as well as lower licence fees and vastly improved fuel consumption of above 60mpg in many cases. The chirpy appearance of the Robin was also a contributory factor in the buoyant sales and this factor was enhanced by the range of nine bright colours available, as follows:

Venetian Blue	April Yellow
London Red	Arctic White
Desert Tan	Tropic Green
Tangerine	Caramel
	Virginia Brown

| . . . with black interior | . . . with tan interior. |

Also in 1975 production of the Robin commenced in Athens at the Mebea Co. where initially 10 cars per week were leaving the line and a target of 1,000 vehicles was set for 1976. A warning note, however, was sounded by *Autocar* magazine, whose comparative performance figures showed how the initial competitiveness of the Robin was beginning to be handicapped by its purchase price.

Model	Price	Weight	cc	0–50mph	Max. mph	mpg
Robin 750	£801	8cwt	747	22.0s	72	50
Mini 850	£692	12cwt	848	25.0s	70	37.6
Fiat 126	£698	11cwt	594	38.0s	68	40.7
Daf 44	£747	14cwt	844	34.3s	73.7	31.3

Throughout the years of Regal production, in its various forms the car had gained the reputation among non-tricar enthusiasts of being ugly, noisy and holding up miles of traffic, with a penchant for performing acrobatics when negotiating corners. However, the new Ogle design offered from Tamworth in the exciting and aerodynamic shape of the Robin undermined many of the previous arguments against this breed of car. Magazine testers found the handling much improved, as well as the performance, allied to enhanced comfort and finish to the interior. The main drawbacks appeared to centre on the noise levels and heating arrangements.

The ease of parking and excellent braking performance made up for the many of the deficiencies of the three-wheeler design.

Within two years in 1975, the capacity of the Reliant all-alloy engine was increased to 850cc, which immediately reduced the 0–60mph acceleration time of the Robin to 17.3sec, accompanied by an increase in fuel economy to 50–60 mpg. The annual road tax figure was now £16 as opposed to £40 for comparable four-wheeled saloons but the purchase price had now reached £1,400, which was partly offset by the potential longevity of the Robin compared with its steel-bodied competitors.

During the late 1970s sales began to flag thanks to a general recession in Britain, and to try and counteract this Reliant decided to sharpen up the body style of the Robin. They accomplished this, literally, by replacing it with the wedge-shaped Rialto model in 1982, incorporating fashionable rectangular headlamps from the Austin Metro. The same basic mechanicals as the Robin were still used but a galvanised chassis was offered to complement the corrosion-resistant bodywork. The price had now reached £2,974 for the saloon and £2,769 for the van version, which was gradually getting closer to the prices of comparable four-wheelers such as the Fiat 126 (£2,995) and the Mini (£4,675). Meanwhile, road tax was now £28 compared with £70 for four-wheeled vehicles. Demand rose slightly as one might expect when a revised model appears on the market, as loyal owners updated their mode of transport to the latest model in the firm expectation of some improvements, which in this instance were mainly cosmetic and equipment based.

In March 1983 Reliant introduced the revised Rialto 2 now fitted with what was termed the HT-E engine. The 'E' referred to the economy aspect of the new variant and involved a rise in compression ratio from 9.5:1 to 10.5:1, which surprisingly reduced the maximum power of the engine from 40bhp to 37.5bhp but increased the torque figure from 46lb/ft to 49.5lb/ft at lower engine revs in each case. This HT-E unit was identified by the use of a yellow rocker cover instead of the usual red variety. However, the more powerful version of the stalwart alloy engine was installed again in September 1986, when the final SE version of the Rialto appeared in the price lists. Seemingly the Rialto did not have the same appeal as its predecessor, so in 1989 the Robin name was revived to complement the Rialto as an up-market version, featuring more rounded styling and again adopting the contemporary Ford Fiesta headlamps. Eventually the Rialto was dropped from the range leaving the Robin as the sole example of the three-wheeled range once more. Various special editions, such as the 93LE and Diamond version, were marketed to stimulate interest among potential buyers. Apart from the traditional customers for the Robin there were some surprisingly prestigious buyers, including HRH the Princess Royal, already a Scimitar GTE owner, who used the three-wheeler around her Gatcombe Park estate in Gloucestershire.

The US embassy in Berkeley Square London was another unlikely customer when they acquired three Robins in 1990 on account of their economy and manoeuvrability in the big city. They even added two more Robins to their fleet in 1998. At this time Reliant was in the hands of Jonathan Heynes, who had plans to introduce a pick-up version, but this model never saw the production line

The neat rear-end styling devised by Ogle for the new Robin, following their success with previous Reliant four-wheeled passenger cars. The three-door opening rear hatch design was the forerunner of a whole new concept adopted subsequently by all the world's car manufacturers, the 'hatchback'. The waist-band coachline moulded into the glass fibre gives an enhanced impression of length.

This brilliant, mobile cutaway version of the new Robin demonstrates very clearly the compact layout of the design. Particularly noteworthy are the chassis uprights behind the front wheel, which afforded greater protection in frontal impacts, as demonstrated in our earlier picture involving a Regal van using similar construction.

The facia of this left-hand-drive example of the Robin illustrates the major improvement in cabin design incorporated by Ogle. The formerly intrusive engine compartment has been absorbed into the facia and the gear shift now sprouts more modestly from under the dashboard in the horizontal position. Note the fresh air vent in the centre and demisting outlets below the screen.

The start of the Robin production line shows the freshly moulded bodyshells about to become united with the rolling chassis. The bucket in the foreground indicates that at this point the bodyshell is rubbed down prior to painting followed by mechanical assembly.

Surely not intended as a comment on the average Robin owner, this chimp at Twycross Zoo is being given a special preview of the new three-wheeler. Nevertheless, it demonstrated that Reliant had a human face. Well, almost . . .

. . . while here, our new delivery boy makes off with the bananas.

This equally posed publicity scene conveys the happy and carefree lifestyle now available to Robin family car owners. Clearly Reliant were aiming at the second car market rather than just ex-motorcyclists needing family transport, who had been their mainstay for many years.

Another publicity shot clearly aimed at the motorcycle user to demonstrate the superior advantages of the Super Robin Estate, in this instance over the motor cycle with pillion passenger seen overtaking it. The same driver's and road fund licences were required for both means of transportation.

A rear view of the Robin Estate de luxe, featuring alloy wheels and rear bumper overriders. Note the low level at which the rear door opens, allowing easy access to the rear load compartment. The radio aerial was positioned as far as possible from the engine to reduce interference.

The Robin van shared the same body mould as the Estate version and was particularly neat in appearance. The driving lights and front overriders indicate that this is the de luxe specification. With a payload of 5cwt the van had a slightly lower rear axle ratio of 3.55:1, as opposed to 3.23:1 for the saloon version.

This fleet of 40 Robin vans intended for the RSPCA was a 150th anniversary gift from Pedigree Pet Foods. The vans were known for their operating economy, ease of driving and parking. The fleet is seen leaving Reliant's Tamworth factory in the spring of 1975.

When the Robin van was introduced in 1973 its annual road fund licence cost just £10 and it could carry a payload of 5cwt. Its 750cc engine achieved between 40 and 60 mpg depending on load and type of journey. Rot-proof bodywork ensured a long service life too.

Freshly painted Robin estate and van body shells emerge from the paintshop prior to fitting the rolling chassis at the Two Gates assembly shop, 1973. Production of the Robin in its first year reached 10,000 and the record rate of 330 per week was reached in March 1974.

The 1977 Robin received some cosmetic updates, such as the front grille now composed of fewer and bolder chrome strips. The engine had been enlarged to 850cc delivering 40bhp and could potentially deliver 60mpg.

A preview for journalists and dealers was arranged for the new Robin at Twycross Zoo in October 1978. The tiger cub is obviously intrigued by the new Robin, or more likely by its tasty occupants, but has been momentarily diverted by its own reflection in the glossy paintwork.

In common with other motor manufacturers, Reliant introduced limited special edition models to encourage sales at slack times. The Jubilee model featured here was introduced in 1977 to coincide with the 25th anniversary of the Queen's accession to the throne. Special colours and alloy wheels were fitted to these versions.

This scene in an Alpine pass emphasises the capabilities of the Robin in winter conditions. The light weight and good rear wheel traction are well up to the demands of winter conditions and the single front wheel reduces resistance to forward motion on snow-covered roads.

This eye-catching harbourside shot attempts to invest the Ogle-styled Robin with the chic and allure of the pleasure boat scene. Its smoothly contoured profile certainly elevated the Robin from the previous image of pure economy motoring.

The interior of the Robin was really quite spacious for such a small car – the compact dimensions of the front seats certainly assisted in making space available for rear-seat occupants. The generous glass area gave excellent all-round visibility.

Take a fresh look at Reliant

The Robin name was reintroduced in 1989 with a new Reliant logo. Although it naturally shared many of the Rialto body panels and chassis, the front styling was more rounded now, using Ford Fiesta headlamps in place of the Austin Metro units used on the Rialto. A shallow front grille and pointed waistline stripes helped to differentiate the new moulding.

The Robin was now a hatchback as it had been in earlier years. LX and GLX versions were offered with varying special paint finishes including Caribbean green and Kingfisher red, as well as additional equipment such as stereo cassette and rear wash/wipe system. The Rialto estate and van continued in parallel production until 1989.

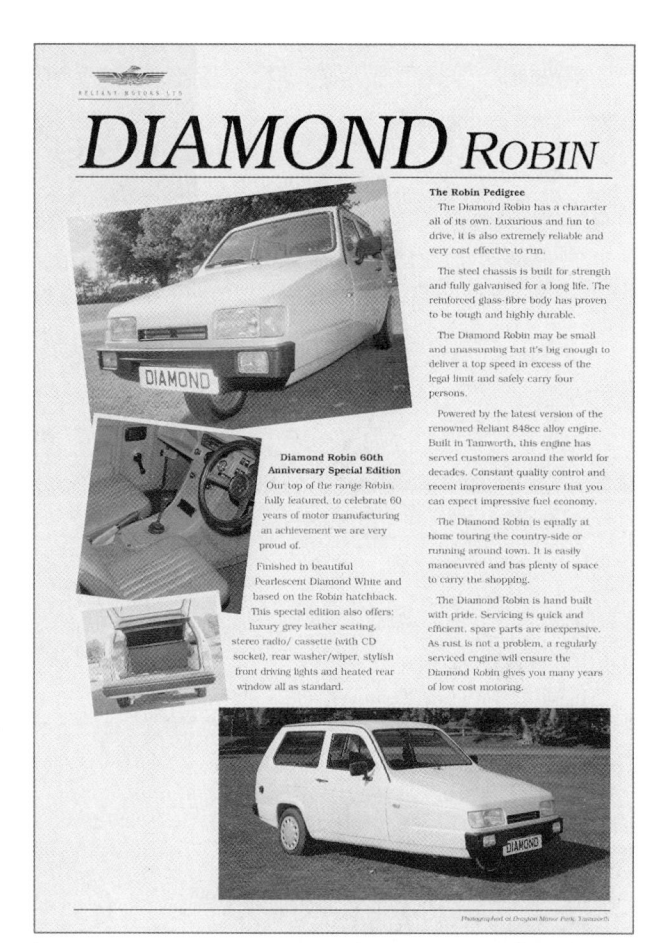

The Diamond Special Edition of the Robin hatchback finished in pearlescent white was introduced in 1985 by the Amex group, which owned Reliant at the time, to celebrate the 60th anniversary of the beginning of Reliant as a company. Grey leather seats and heated rear window were unique features on this new model.

1993 saw the arrival of another 'limited edition', the LE 93, the numeral signifying the year of production. 1993 must have been as good a year to celebrate as any. Most evident were the special colour flashes applied to the sills and bonnet in either red with brown or blue with yellow-on-white bodywork.

This view of the bonnet of the LE93 'special' shows the paint details distinguishing this model at the front. Such 'limited editions' are deemed necessary by most motor manufacturers in promoting sales, although in this case the basic vehicle and running gear were retained unchanged with no obvious development.

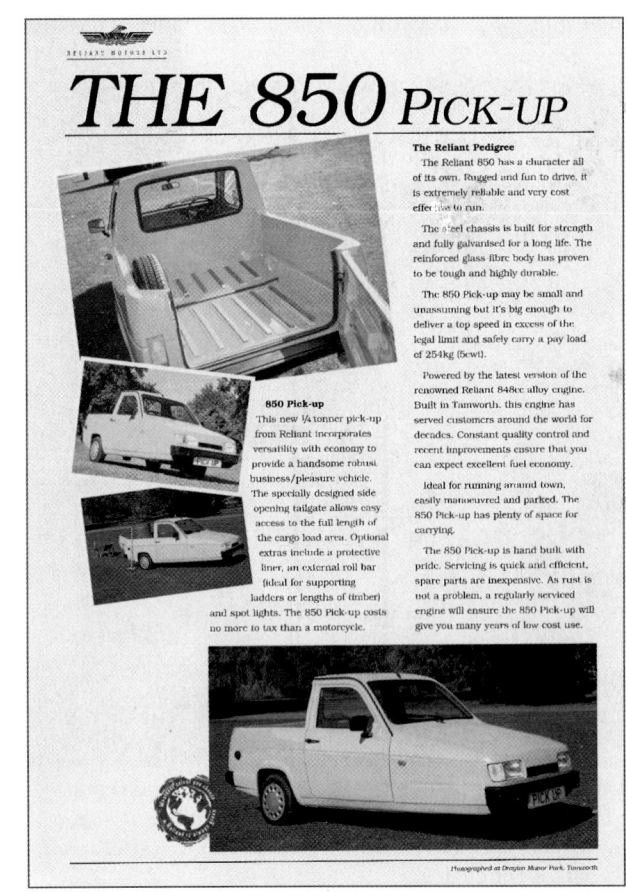

THE 850 PICK-UP

The Reliant Pedigree

The Reliant 850 has a character all of its own. Rugged and fun to drive, it is extremely reliable and very cost effective to run.

The steel chassis is built for strength and fully galvanised for a long life. The reinforced glass-fibre body has proven to be tough and highly durable.

The 850 Pick-up may be small and unassuming but it's big enough to deliver a top speed in excess of the legal limit and safely carry a pay load of 254kg (5cwt).

Powered by the latest version of the renowned Reliant 848cc alloy engine. Built in Tamworth, this engine has served customers around the world for decades. Constant quality control and recent improvements ensure that you can expect excellent fuel economy.

Ideal for running around town, easily manoeuvred and parked. The 850 Pick-up has plenty of space for carrying.

The 850 Pick-up is hand built with pride. Servicing is quick and efficient, spare parts are inexpensive. As rust is not a problem, a regularly serviced engine will ensure the 850 Pick-up will give you many years of low cost use.

850 Pick-up

This new ¼ tonner pick-up from Reliant incorporates versatility with economy to provide a handsome robust business/pleasure vehicle. The specially designed side opening tailgate allows easy access to the full length of the cargo load area. Optional extras include a protective liner, an external roll bar (ideal for supporting ladders or lengths of timber) and spot lights. The 850 Pick-up costs no more to tax than a motorcycle.

Photographed at Drayton Manor Park, Tamworth

When Jonathan Heynes took over the running of Reliant in 1996, he had ideas for expanding the range of 3-wheelers, including reviving the 5cwt pick-up version, now known as the 850, which had originally been listed when the Robin was first introduced but apparently never went into production. Very few of this latest version were made either, as Heynes enjoyed only a limited tenure of the company.

The Robin van was a logical model for Reliant to produce in line with previous ranges and was a simple variant of the hatchback saloon. These were extremely useful town delivery vehicles, being purchased by the US embassy in London and the Princess Royal for her Gatcombe estate, to complement her Scimitar GTE.

The latest manifestation of the Robin was introduced in late 1995 and featured a more rounded frontal aspect incorporating Vauxhall Corsa headlamps. The redesigned front grille and bumper moulding was much more aerodynamic, which may have assisted greater speed and economy despite the lack of any development of the chassis or engine.

dealerships while retaining the established qualities of economy and long life of the Regal range.

The appropriately named Rebel shared most of its running gear with its three-wheeled stable mates, but the independent coil spring front suspension was 'borrowed' from the Standard 10, together with the Burman worm and nut steering mechanism. The light weight, at 10.5cwt, allowed the 27bhp engine to endow the Rebel with a reasonably competitive performance at a selling price of £524. However, the relatively bland body shape and its modest engine size limited its sales potential, so Reliant responded in 1967 by enlarging the engine to 700cc which increased the power output to 30bhp for an extra £100 list price. An estate version was added to the range, and when tested by *Autocar* magazine in 1968 produced the following comparative performance figures:

Model	cc	Price	Max. mph	0–60 mph	mpg
Rebel 700	700	£624	68	35.9s	40
Hillman Husky	875	£698	76	24.2s	35
Mini Estate	998	£672	76	26.2s	40
Renault 4	845	£618	72	32.1s	40

Four years later a further enlargement of the engine to 750cc took place, increasing the power output by only 1bhp as a result of a reduction in compression ratio from 8.4:1 to 7.5:1, which increased the torque figure to maintain fuel economy. The maximum speed did increase – to 75mph – but so did the selling price, which now stood at £861 for the saloon and £931 for the estate version. Production of the Rebel ceased in 1974 after a relatively modest 3,500 examples had left Tamworth. The reason given was to permit expansion of the Robin three-wheeler, which continued to sell well. Undeterred by the relatively poor sales of the Rebel, Reliant commissioned Ogle to design a replacement and this resulted in the Kitten, introduced in 1975. The bodyshell was virtually a Robin passenger cabin with a revised front end to accommodate the four-wheel layout. Thus the rear opening window and rear lights were similar to those fitted to the Robin as well as the doors and windows, which reduced development costs somewhat. The chassis, however, was entirely different from that of the Rebel, consisting of straighter box sections which were simple to construct, and independent coil spring front suspension which now employed Triumph Herald components, including rack and pinion steering.

This latter feature not only endowed the Kitten with far more positive steering but also an incredible 23ft turning circle, 1 ft less than a London taxi! This ability was featured in one of the car's adverts. By this time the venerable all-alloy Reliant engine fitted to the contemporary Robin had a capacity of 850cc, so naturally the Kitten was also powered by this 40bhp unit. However, the Kitten now faced even stronger competition than the Rebel because of the progress made by other manufacturers in this field, and the *Autocar* road test figures illustrate this:

Model	cc	Price	0–60 mph	Max. mph	mpg
Kitten	848	£1499	19.6s	78	41.5
Imp	875	£1345	21.1s	80	32.4
Fiat 127	903	£1434	17.4s	83	32.0
Mini 1000	998	£1332	18.7s	82	34.2

While the Kitten was marginally more expensive than its rivals it more than compensated by its superior fuel economy, most road testers commenting that it was quite difficult to achieve less than 50mpg in normal motoring. This aspect was emphasised by a standard model winning its class in the 1976 Mobil Economy run by achieving an overall consumption of 55.11mpg. Of course, the Kitten also had the potential of longevity because of its rust-proof bodywork and relatively cheap maintenance costs. Reliant added to its desirability by offering heated rear window and rear window wash-wipe system as optional extras allied to an attractive range of nine body colours. Naturally an estate version was added to the range from the outset, again using the rear bodywork of the Robin Estate, which made a very balanced and useful vehicle offering 35 cubic feet of luggage space when the rear seats were folded down, compared with a creditable 30 cu. ft for the saloon version.

The resale price of the Kitten rose to £1,670 by 1977, with the Estate version selling for £2,134 and even the van version costing £1,821. Gradually the cost of producing the Kitten by hand rendered it less competitive, and the model was finally dropped in 1982 after about 4,500 had been made. However, the design was not totally redundant as a licence was granted to an Indian manufacturer to continue production of what was known as the Dolphin. A pick-up version of the Kitten was already in production in India, known as the Fox, and Reliant decided to see if this model had some potential in the UK. Thus in 1983 three versions of the Fox were added to the price lists in this country, namely the Utility costing £3,507, the Pick-up and Hardtop both selling at £3,593. Probably because of the lack of any advertising effort only 601 examples of the Fox were sold here by the time production ceased in 1990.

It is certainly debatable whether Reliant should ever have pursued the four-wheeled route in their economy range despite their success with the totally different Scimitar model. From the very beginning Reliant had dominated the limited but adequate three-wheeler market which matched their production abilities perfectly. The niche market they occupied had and still has potential as the 'town car', where manoeuvrability and economy are at a premium. However, the method of hand production imposed on Reliant would increasingly be a handicap economically and so the company has taken the decision to import vehicles from Europe to compete in this market.

Variations on a theme

One potential market for their four-wheeler design that Reliant chose for whatever reason not to follow-up was the small 'ragtop' sports car sector, today booming again thanks to the Mazda MX-5 and BMW Z3. During the mid-1980s the production of British open two-seater sports cars virtually ceased except for specialist concerns such as Morgan and Caterham. A number of designers had viewed the Kitten chassis as a potential basis for a new British sports car on the lines of the Austin-Healey 'Frogeye' Sprite, most notably Tony Stevens. His first attempt at producing such a car was the Sienna, which had separate flowing mudguards very much in the Morgan image. Only one example was made, which still exists. He then designed a very attractive car also based on the Kitten chassis and running gear called the Cipher, styled on the lines of the lamented Lotus Elan. Despite glowing reports by *Motor* magazine and other publications Reliant decided it was too expensive to manufacture, and followed an altogether different route involving outside component suppliers and designers to produce the Scimitar SS1, with disastrous sales results. A less ambitious project by a Lancashire engineer involved fitting a MG TD-type glass fibre body to a slightly modified Kitten chassis. This was called the Tempest and twenty-three of these were assembled, apparently with the approval of Reliant. A private project by Iain Daniels of Stroud, Gloucestershire, to produce a trials special on a Rebel chassis on the lines of the Lotus Seven again shows the potential of the Reliant running gear, which unfortunately the manufacturers chose to ignore. Neither the Rebel nor the Kitten could be considered failures but the competition was too great for their production and development to be sustained. At least they did not encroach on their established three-wheeler market, which mainly consisted of super-loyal enthusiasts for this mode of transport.

Ray Wiggin was not only responsible for the sucessful new ranges of three-wheelers but was keen to expand the Reliant market into small four-wheeled passenger and commercial vehicles which could share power units and many body panels with the existing well-established three-wheeled designs.

Reliant Rebel: a cutaway view

The otherwise conventional layout of the Rebel was based on a completely new chassis. Front independent coil spring suspension was 'borrowed' from the Standard 10, as was the steering mechanism. The engine was the same 600cc unit as in the contemporary Regal 3/30 but changes in the valve sizes and cylinder head clearance raised the power from 21 to 27bhp to counter the extra weight.

A cutaway model of the Rebel clearly shows the front coil spring suspension and steering mechanism from the Standard 10. The stout chassis and separate glass fibre body gave the car quite a high ride height but also a potentially long life.

This production line scene from 1965 gives the impression of a successful model rolling off the line at the rate of one a minute. Sadly the Rebel was not the moneyspinner Reliant had hoped for, as it was selling in a very competitive area of the car market where unit profits were never high in the first place.

Reliant's waterproof testing bay might easily be mistaken for a car wash! Each model was subjected to this treatment, as all the vehicles were hand built and thus subject to occasional sealing problems associated with accuracy of assembly.

Another publicity shot of the family picnic attempts to convey the commodious nature of the Reliant Rebel, with accommodation for two adults and three children. The design combined the space of the average 1100cc car with the economy of a 700cc engine.

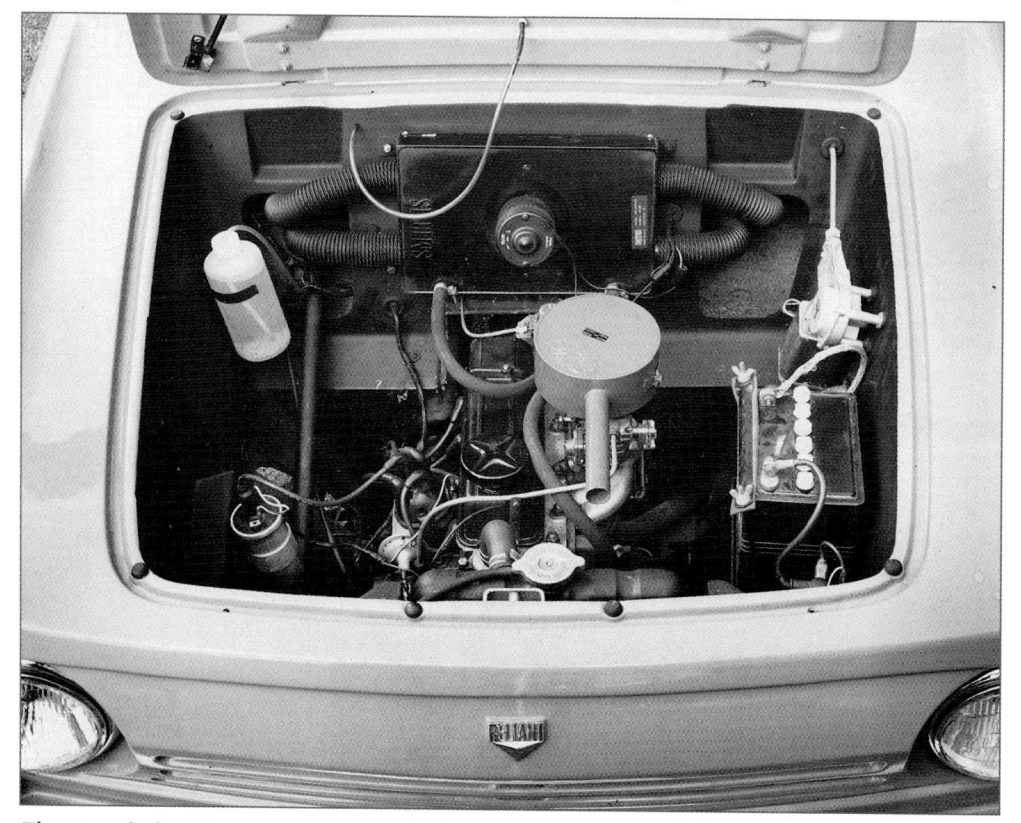

The tiny, light alloy engine seems to have quite disappeared beneath the clutter in this underbonnet view of the Rebel. Accessibility to all the major serviceable components was good, however – a critical factor as most Reliant owners tended to do their own maintenance.

The Rebel proved an ideal vehicle for economy competitions owing to its light weight and small engine capacity. This scene during the 1967 Mobil Economy Run shows the variety of cars used by competitors, including a Ford Zodiac Mk II behind the Rebel.

In the same 1967 Mobil Economy Run this particular Rebel saloon driven by Brian Smith achieved an overall consumption figure of 51mpg. This would have given him overall victory had he not inadvertently left the road on the tricky moorland stage seen here. The resulting body damage eliminated the Reliant from the results.

An estate van version of the Rebel, with a very neat appearance, was a useful addition to the range. To cater for the increased load carrying requirement the engine size was increased to 700cc in 1967 and finally to 750cc in 1972, giving 32bhp.

The 700cc Rebel model featured this sophisticated moulded dashboard, which included a temperature gauge as well as the usual speedo and fuel gauge. The useful parcel shelf below the dashboard complemented a lockable glove box in front of the passenger. Door trims and seats were well finished for an economy car.

This rear view of the Kitten hatchback shows the 30 cu. ft luggage space available when the rear seats were folded down.

The standard Kitten was fitted with steel wheels and chrome hubcaps as opposed to the optional alloy items. A spare wheel cover was available as an option costing £3.90 and a load area mat at £4.70 was also offered. Other options included a laminated windscreen, heated rear screen, a reclining passenger seat and a radio.

This punning publicity picture emphasizes the spacious rear compartment of the Kitten. Any association between cars and animals would hardly be politically correct in today's climate, and would probably result in a raid by RSPCA commandos!

A Kitten posed outside Castle Howard in Yorkshire, the exotic setting for Granada TV's *Brideshead Revisited*. The then owner, Mr George Howard, already had a Scimitar GTE. Presumably Reliant felt the Kitten might make an ideal partner to the GTE for estate work as it had at Gatcombe Park.

kitten

Runs rings round other cars.
The car built to stay young.

The Kitten estate boasted a remarkably tight turning circle on full lock of only 23 feet, a foot less than the official specification of a London taxicab. This was thanks to the adoption of the Triumph Herald front suspension and steering rack.

Ray Wiggin (left), Managing Director of Reliant, congratulating Malcolm Young and his co-driver on winning their class in the 1976 Total Economy Drive. At this time the Reliant management were very supportive of any owners' efforts to demonstrate the abilities of their products.

A moorland scene on the 1976 Total Economy Drive, showing the difficult terrain over which the event was run. Even so, this class-winning Kitten driven by Malcolm Young achieved 55 mpg overall. The lightweight and efficient alloy engine proved its worth time and again in this competition.

Naturally Reliant produced a van version of the Kitten for small contractors as well as for dual-purpose family use. It was far more economical than rival vehicles and lasted much longer, thanks to its rust-free glass fibre construction.

The Fox was effectively a pick-up version of the Kitten and was introduced initially in Greece. Reliant chose to include it in the UK market in 1983 after Kitten production had ceased. It was available in open, hard-top and soft-top versions.

For some reason Reliant never produced a Kitten pick-up but the belated introduction of the Fox was a worthwhile move. So little publicity was given to the model, however, that only 600 were sold between 1983 and 1990, priced at £3,500–£3,600 depending on equipment level.

5
Of Beatles and Bugs

Four illustrations showing how the concept of the Bond Bug developed with Ogle Design. The idea was first conceived ten years previously by Ogle boss, Tom Karen, but it was not until 1970 that an opportunity arose for the idea to become reality.

The Reliant products covered by this chapter are quite different in character, price and application yet are still based on the well-established, three-wheeled theme. The Ant was specifically a commercial vehicle, true to the traditions from which the Reliant company originated. The Bug on the other hand could not be more extreme in that it was a fun vehicle intended for the young buyer as a modern means of transport for two people. The common theme linking these two diverse concepts is that both were designed by Ogle who had such good relations with Reliant at this time.

*

The Ant, or TW9 as it was known in Reliant circles, was originally developed with the Mediterranean and Middle Eastern countries in view. Greece in particular ordered 250 left-hand-drive versions following the successful marketing of the Regal chassis cab derived from the Regal van. The overseas left-hand-drive version had a carrying capacity of only 10cwt but Reliant reckoned that a larger load capacity would be required for the Ant to sell well in Britain. Thus the UK versions of the Ant had a 16cwt load capacity, which was asking quite a lot of the 700cc, 27.5bhp alloy engine fitted at its introduction in 1967. Despite this the top speed of the Ant was reckoned to be 54mph giving a fuel

By 1973 the engine capacity of the TW9, subsequently known as the Ant, was increased to 750cc, giving a power output of 32bhp. The payload was now 16cwt and so carrying a Reliant Regal weighing only 8 cwt must have been well within its capability, making it an ideal recovery vehicle for a Reliant dealer.

Reliant TW9 Ants being assembled at Mebea in Greece. This turned out to be the main export market for this useful vehicle. Initially about 400 were exported in a finished state before assembly started locally using kits exported by Reliant.

Opposite: Yet another application of the versatile TW9 or Ant is this tipper christened the 'Munibug', used for refuse collection. The hydraulic arm was powered by a pump driven by belt from the gearbox of the main power unit. This was possible because the arm was only used when the vehicle was stationary.

Showing off every tiny detail, this stripped-down Motor Show exhibit is the final version of the model shown below, now fitted with coil spring suspension for a firmer ride all round. The rear suspension was the only mechanical deviation from the other Reliant three-wheeler vehicles. The Bug was, of course, ideal beach-wear.

This behind-the-scenes shot of the Motor Show exhibit being prepared shows how neatly the various mechanical components of the Bond Bug integrated with the Ogle design. Making the moulded seats part of the rear bodywork was particularly clever, saving weight and adding strength. No springs have been fitted at this stage of construction.